Tap in a Pan!

Written by Sue Graves

Collins

Tap, tap, tap it.

Pit, pit, pat it.

Dip it in.

Sit in it.

Tap in it.

It is a tin pan.

Dip in a tin.

Tip it!

A man dips it in.

It tips. It is dim.

Is a man in it?

A man is in it!

Dip, tip, tap

tap it

dip it

tap it

tip it

dip it

a man in it

Ideas for reading

Written by Clare Dowdall, PhD
Lecturer and Primary Literacy Consultant

Learning objectives: *(reading objectives correspond with Pink A band; all other objectives correspond with White band)* read simple words by sounding out and blending the phonemes all through the word from left to right; draw together ideas and information from across a whole text; explain ideas and processes using imaginative and adventurous vocabulary and non-verbal gestures to support communication

Curriculum links: Geography

Focus phonemes: s, a, t, p, i, n, m, d

Resources: internet

Word count: 48

Getting started

- Explain to children that they will be learning about festivals. Ask them to name any special celebrations and festivals that they know. Look at the picture on the front cover and ask children to describe what they can see and how this picture relates to the book's title.

- Look at the words in the title together. Add sound buttons to each phoneme in each word and practise blending the sounds in the words to read them.

- Turn to the blurb. Ask children to read the text aloud. Support them to blend the sounds in the word *d-i-p* and then reread the text fluently.

Reading and responding

- Turn to pp2–3. Model how to read the text using the commas to pause.

- Ask children to describe what is happening at this celebration. Support them to give detailed information and use adventurous vocabulary.

- Ask children to read to p13 independently. Encourage them to blend phonemes to read new words, and to reread each sentence fluently following blending. Listen as children read.